Lulu Mayo

HOW TO DRAW A
BUNNY
AND OTHER CUTE CREATURES

WITH SIMPLE SHAPES
IN 5 STEPS

Andrews McMeel
PUBLISHING®

FROM LULU

I hope you love cute critters as much as I do. Inside this book, I'll show you how to draw lots of sweet animals, including guinea pigs, chicks, puppies, and, of course, bunnies.

Each adorable creature is brought to life in five simple steps, using shapes that are easy to master. Don't worry if you make a mistake or your pictures look different from mine—all drawings are unique, and that's part of what makes them special. Have fun!

LULU MAYO

THE STEPS

The clear, step-by-step instructions for
each creation in this book are easy to follow.

Outlining the body gives
you a great starting point.
Use a pencil to create
your initial drawing.

Add simple shapes to
start bringing your
character to life.

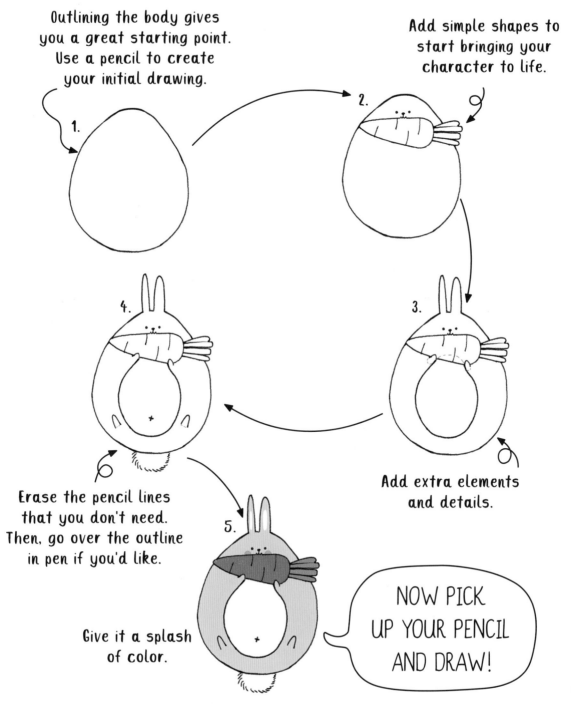

Erase the pencil lines
that you don't need.
Then, go over the outline
in pen if you'd like.

Add extra elements
and details.

Give it a splash
of color.

NOW PICK
UP YOUR PENCIL
AND DRAW!

GUINEA PIG

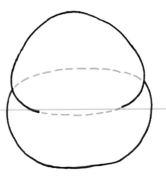

1. start with two ovals for
the head and body

2. add eyes, nose,
mouth, and oval ears

3. add a bunch of flowers
and triangle paws

4. big bow and oval feet

5. add markings and
a pop of color

Give it a go here. ↰

2

Draw more plump guinea pigs here. Try starting with various shapes to create different guinea pig poses.

Is it edible, Mr. Guinea Pig?

MACARONODILE

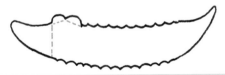

1. start with a curved triangle for the face, semicircle eyes, and a spiky triangle body

2. add a line for the mouth, dots for eyes and nose, and rectangles for legs

3. semicircles and fluffy rectangles make the macaron

4. add triangle spikes on the tail

5. color your favorite flavor

Now you try.

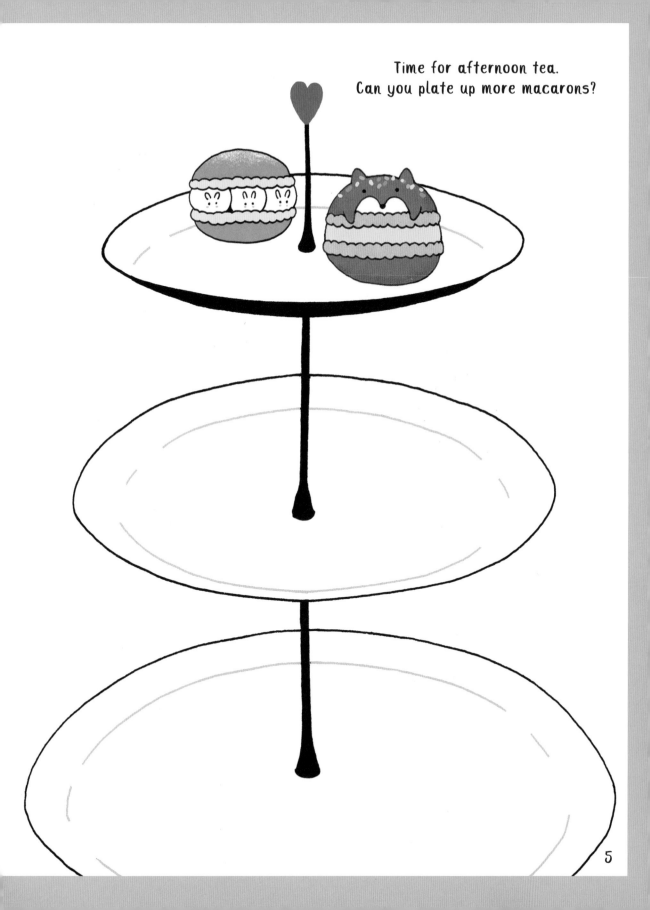

Time for afternoon tea.
Can you plate up more macarons?

BUNNY

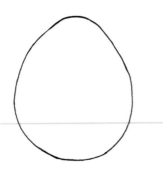

1. egg shape for the body

2. add eyes, a nose, a triangle for the carrot, and rectangles for the stalk

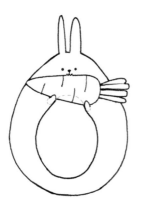

3. long ears and ovals for the belly and paws

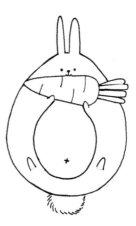

4. add triangle legs, a fluffy tail, and a belly button

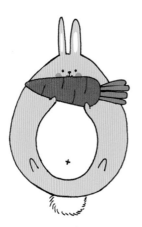

5. give it a splash of color

Your turn.

6

Fill the field with cute bunnies. You can
draw them any shape you want.

DEER

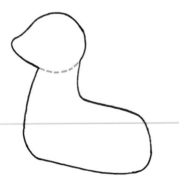

1. teardrop for the head
and an L-shaped body

2. add an eye, teardrop ear,
and a heart for the nose

3. triangles for legs

4. add spots and a
leaf-shaped tail

5. finish with color

Draw your deer.

8

Use these shapes to try out different poses.

Come here, deer!

All male deer—
apart from the
Chinese water
deer—have antlers.

DUCKLING

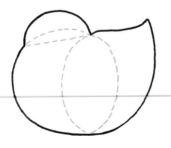

1. semicircle head with a circle and teardrop for the body

2. draw the beak and dots for eyes

3. a zigzag for the eggshell

4. add a hat and a flower

5. color it up

Have a go here.

Use these shapes to create your very own duck family.

Rubber duckie

He doesn't say much.

LADYBUG

1. eye-shaped face,
a big eye, and horn

2. antennae and oval
for the body

3. draw the shell line
and zigzags for legs

4. add spots and belly lines

5. finish with a
flourish of color

Draw yours.

Fill the page with more lovely ladybugs and clover leaves.

GROUNDHOG MUFFIN

1. ovals for the head and
ear and lines for the body

2. add a hat, a bow tie, triangles
for paws, and dots for the face

3. a wobbly oval and rounded
rectangle make the muffin

4. draw fur, sprinkles,
and patterns on the wrapper

5. color and decorate

Your turn.

Can you draw a groundhog family peeking out of a muffin
or a groundhog popping out of another sweet treat?

KOALA

1. oval for the head and fluffy
clouds for the ears

2. add nose and large dots
for the eyes

3. circle for the back

4. chubby triangle arm,
oval leg, and a sausage foot

5. add a flower
and color it up

It's your turn.

16

Can you complete the scene with more flowers and cute koalas?

Draw a baby koala here.

LAMB SUSHI

1. start with a
flat rectangle and a
fluffy rectangle

2. add eyes and a nose

3. tall, curved rectangle
and triangle legs

4. oval ears

5. add color

Try it out.

Use this page to prepare more sushi animals. Or experiment
with shapes to create different lamb poses.

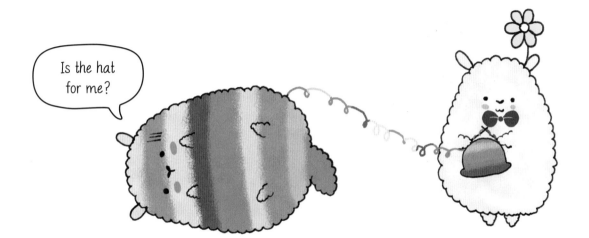

CHOCOLATE BUNNY

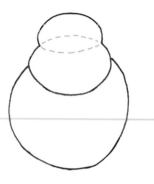

1. two ovals for the head
and a crescent for the body

2. large eyes, nose, and
semicircles for feet

3. ovals for ears
and a flower crown

4. add a bow and
strokes for the fur

5. color your
chocolate creation

Hop to it!

Create your collection of yummy chocolate bunnies here.

You'll never eat me, will you?

SLOW LORIS

1. carrot shape and oval for the body

2. draw a cute facial expression

3. semicircle ear and chubby triangle arm and leg

4. add the stalk and lines on the carrot

5. pick a bold color

Have a go!

These slow lorises love carrots.
Can you draw more of them having fun?

As they are nocturnal animals,
slow lorises need big eyes
to be able to see at night.

LLAMA BUNNY

1. fluffy, L-shaped body

2. fluffy circle for the face and dots for the eyes and nose

3. add a bow and ovals to make long bunny ears

4. fluffy triangles for legs and a fluffy oval for the tail

5. add rainbow colors

Give it a go.

Use these shapes to create your own llama band.
Can you draw a llama playing a tambourine?

Shake shake

CATERPILLAR

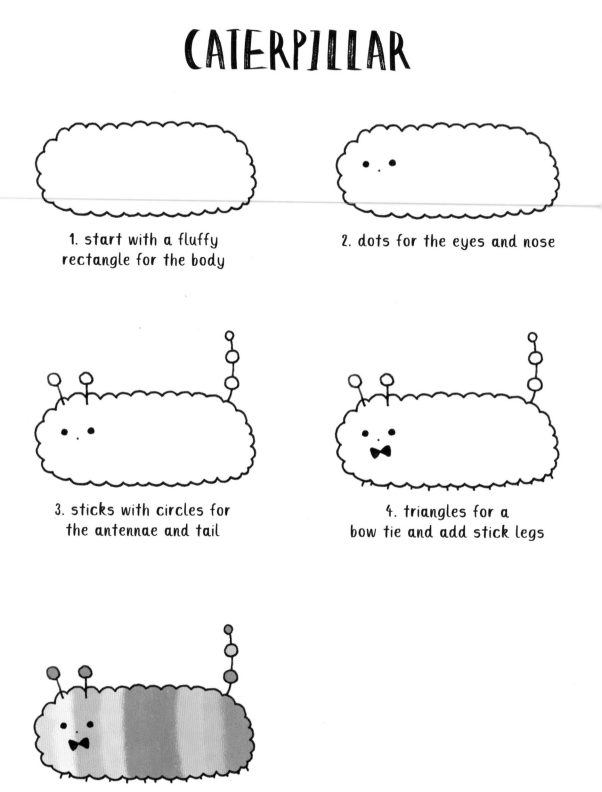

1. start with a fluffy
rectangle for the body

2. dots for the eyes and nose

3. sticks with circles for
the antennae and tail

4. triangles for a
bow tie and add stick legs

5. finish with stripes of color

Try it out.

Fill this page with more adorable caterpillars.

Do you like
my new shoes?

RACCOON RABBIT

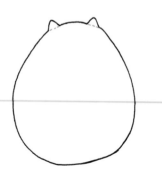

1. oval body and triangle ears

2. heart-shaped face, eyes,
T for the nose, and oval bunny ears

3. triangles for the arms and
legs and a circle for the belly

4. add a belly button, a
triangle, and a bushy tail

5. add color to the
raccoon in disguise

Now you try.

**Fill the page with squishy raccoons.
How about a dumpling-shaped raccoon?**

Yoga
raccoon

Floppy raccoon

Hungry raccoon

BEETLE

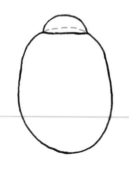

1. semicircle head and an oval for the body

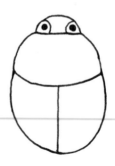

2. big eyes and a T for the wing case

3. mandibles and antennae

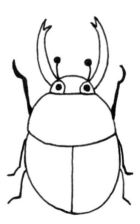

4. add six stick legs

5. dress it up any way you like

Try it out.

How many different beetles can you draw here?

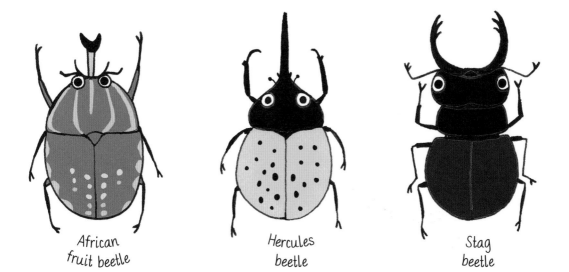

African
fruit beetle

Hercules
beetle

Stag
beetle

BIRD'S NEST

1. scribble a crescent nest

2. add ovals for eggs

3. a teardrop-shaped
body, fluffy circle for a
pom-pom, and a triangle beak

4. draw the eye, cheek, back,
and a heart-shaped wing

5. make it bright
and colorful

Your turn.

Help these birds build their home. Draw more birds,
nests, and trees to complete the scene.

BUMBLEBEE

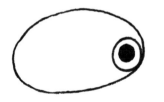

1. start with an oval
body and a big eye

2. add stripes and antennae

3. a heart for the left wing and
a teardrop for the right wing

4. stick legs, stinger,
and a tambourine

5. make it bright
and colorful

Now you draw one here.

These busy bumblebees are collecting nectar.
Help them by drawing more friends and flowers.

DONKEY

1. fluffy oval for hair and
ovals for the head and body

2. add a face
and ovals for ears

3. draw triangles for the
legs and add a bow tie

4. add a cart with flowers

5. finish with color

Sketch yours here.

Fill the field with more cute donkeys.

BASKET OF CHICKS

1. start with a rounded rectangle outline for the basket, then add flowers

2. draw fluffy ovals for the chicks, then add eyes, beaks, and triangle wings

3. fill in the basket

4. add a semicircle handle

5. finish with color

Have a go.

Fill the basket with fluffy chicks. Don't forget to decorate it, too.

DORMOUSE

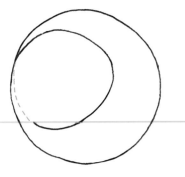

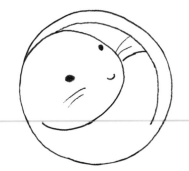

1. start with two circles
for the head and body

2. draw the eyes, nose, whiskers,
and a semicircle for the tail

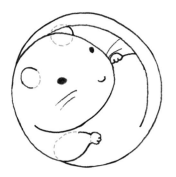

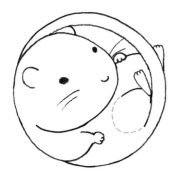

3. circles for ears, oval for
the arm, and two hands

4. an oval for the leg
and add two feet

5. use warm colors
to make it fluffy

Your turn.

Use these shapes to create more a-dor-able dormice.

There's no more food. We might as well sleep.

Dormice can sleep for up to seven months a year.

BUNNY CAT

1. start with an oval for the body

2. add triangle ears and legs

3. eyes, nose, whiskers,
and a fluffy tail

4. add oval bunny
ears and a bow tie

5. color it happy

Now you try!

Fill the page with fancy kitties. How about a kitty
with a bonnet or a beautiful flower headband?

I've got something
for you.

DINO EGG

1. two ovals for the head,
two lines for the shoulders,
and an eggshell hat

2. semicircle and a zigzag
for the shell base

3. add eyes, nose, tummy, and a
curvy triangle for the mouth

4. rectangles for teeth
and triangle arms

5. a pop of color and dino's
ready to see the world

Showtime!

44

Create your very own dino egg family here.

CORGI PUPPY

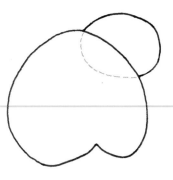

1. oval for the head and
a heart-shaped body

2. add eyes, nose, mouth,
and triangles for ears

3. a fluffy circle for the tail

4. draw a carrot
and a bow tie

5. add adorable color

Sketch yours here.

Fill the page with loveable corgis.

Party time!

BUNNY DOUGHNUT

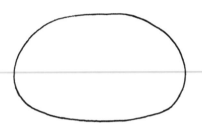

1. long oval for the doughnut

2. ovals for bunny ears

3. eyes, nose, and mouth

4. add dripping glaze

5. decorate and color it up

Draw your doughnut here.

Can you fill the shelves with different flavors of doughnuts?

BABY SEAL

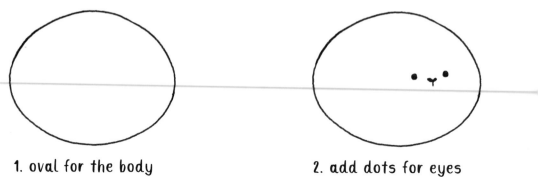

1. oval for the body

2. add dots for eyes
and a heart nose

3. curved line for the chin and
a semicircle for the flipper

4. add a bow and hearts
for the other flipper and tail

5. finish with color

Sketch a seal here.

50

Use these shapes to draw more baby seals having fun under the sea.

It's a seal-abration!

BUTTERFLY

1. long, tilted oval
for the body

2. add a big eye and stripes

3. a heart-shaped
wing and antennae

4. draw legs, a
triangle, and a stick

5. add a splash of color

Better try your own butterfly.

52

Fill the sky with more butterflies.
Add oval wings to create a dragonfly
or triangle wings to make a moth.

UNICORN

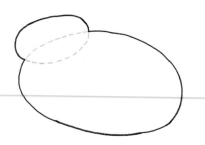

1. ovals for the head and body

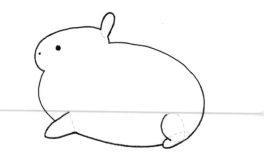

2. eye, nose, a triangle for the front leg, and ovals for the back leg

3. fluffy clouds for the hair and a triangle horn

4. add an egg and a rabbit tail

5. finish with rainbow colors

Your turn.

Doodle some unicorns here. Can you use
the left shape to create a flying unicorn?

Can we swap,
PLEASE?

CARROT

1. rounded, upside-down
triangle for the body

2. add a cute face and
triangles for hands

3. rectangles make the stalk

4. add a bow tie and wrinkles

5. finish with color

Sketch yours here.

Can you grow more carrots in this veggie patch?

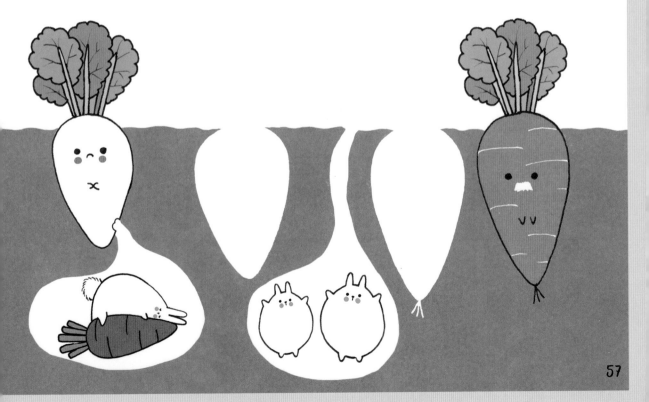

FLOWER

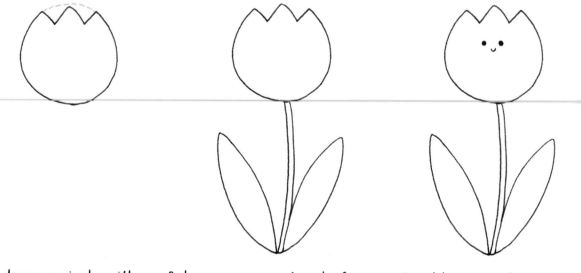

1. draw a circle with
   a zigzag at the top

2. long, wavy rectangle for
   the stem and oval leaves

3. add a cute face

4. draw pollen
   and a pattern

5. add color—
   this one's a tulip

Have a go.

Complete the bouquet with your own flowers.
Don't forget to color them in, too.

SLOTH

1. banana-shaped body

2. triangles for arms

3. heart-shaped face
and a cute expression

4. add claws and a
giant Easter egg

5. decorate the egg
any way you like

Now you try!

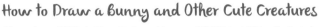

How to Draw a Bunny and Other Cute Creatures

Andrews McMeel Publishing
a division of Andrews McMeel Universal
1130 Walnut Street, Kansas City, Missouri 64106
www.andrewsmcmeel.com

First published in Great Britain in 2021
by Michael O'Mara Books, Ltd.
9 Lion Yard, Tremadoc Road, London SW4 7NQ

21 22 23 24 25 RLP 10 9 8 7 6 5 4 3 2 1

ISBN: 978-1-5248-6501-6
Library of Congress Control Number:
2021945529

Made by:
Shenzhen Reliance Printing Co., Ltd
Address and location of manufacturer:
25 Longshan Industrial Zone, Nanling,
Longgang District, Shenzhen, China, 518114
1st printing—11/16/20

W www.lulumayo.com   f @lulumayoart   @lulu_mayo_art

Writers: Lulu Mayo and Imogen Currell-Williams
Cover Design: John Bigwood
Designer: Jack Clucas
Editor: Jean Z. Lucas
Art Director: Diane Marsh
Production Manager: Tamara Haus
Production Editor: Jasmine Lim

ATTENTION: SCHOOLS AND BUSINESSES
Andrews McMeel books are available at quantity discounts with bulk purchase for
educational, business, or sales promotional use. For information, please e-mail the Andrews
McMeel Publishing Special Sales Department: specialsales@amuniversal.com.

Experiment with these shapes to create your own sloths.

Stretchy sloth

Square sloth

Flower-loving sloth